Acknowledgments

The author and publishers wish to thank the following
for permission to use copyright material:

Alpha Photographic and Press Agency: page 42 (bottom);
Country Life Books: pages 9, 12, 15, 37 (bottom), 40 (bottom);
Gerry Cranham Colour Library: page 44 (top right);
Getty Images: pages 4 (top), 6 (bottom), 10, 13, 14 (bottom), 17,
25 (top left and right), 26 (top left and right, bottom right), 27 (3),
28 (top), 29 (2), 30 (top), 31 (bottom), 32 and back cover,
24 (2), 35 (top), 36, 38 (2), 39 (nos 4, 5, 6, 8), 40 (top), 42 (top),
43, 44 (top left), 45 (top), 50 (top), 51 (top);
Tim Graham Picture Library: cover, front endpaper (left),
and pages 39 (no 7), 41, 46 (2), 47 (2), 48 (2), 49 (2),
50 (bottom), 51 (bottom) and back cover; Imperial War Museum:
pages 14 (top), 16 (top), 18 (top); Keith Logan: title page and page 8;
J McDonald: page 45 (bottom) and back cover; Katz Pictures Ltd:
pages 11 (bottom) and back cover, 22, 24, 28 (bottom), 33 (nos 1
and 4); National Portrait Gallery: pages 6 (top), 7, 18 (bottom), 19;
Popperfoto: page 33 (nos 2, 3, and 5); R M Powell: back endpaper –
family tree; Kevin Rook: pages 20, 39 (no 3); Royal Scottish
Academy of Music and Drama: page 44 (bottom);
Scotsman Features: page 37 (top); John Scott – courtesy of
Mrs Judy Applebee: back cover, front endpaper (right) and pages 5,
35 (bottom); Telegraph Colour Library: page 4 (bottom right).

Published by Ladybird Books Ltd
80 Strand, London, WC2R ORL
A Penguin Company

2 4 6 8 10 9 7 5 3 1

© LADYBIRD BOOKS LTD MCMXCMMII

Printed in Italy

HM QUEEN ELIZABETH

The Queen Mother

by
IAN MORRISON MA PhD

Ladybird

The 20th century has brought some of the greatest changes the human race has ever experienced. The story of the lady best known to us now as the Queen Mother began with the century, and matches it in its blend of tragedies, delights and sheer surprises.

An early photograph of the Queen Mother

Since her birth in 1900, the number of people on Earth has more than doubled, but in other ways the world has shrunk dramatically. When the Queen Mother was little, steam boats and trains were the fastest ways of getting around the world. The first flight by a powered aircraft was still three years off when she was born, yet she was to see men walk upon the Moon. To her parents the television set

After morning service at Windsor

upon which she watched the astronauts would have seemed as unlikely a piece of science fiction as the notion of leaving the Earth by rocket... something out of storybooks by Jules Verne or H G Wells *(far left)*, not something that might actually happen during their daughter's lifetime.

5

An old Scots song tells of 'a lad who was *born* to be king' (though that Prince Charlie fled 'Over the Sea to Skye', and never became a monarch). The baby girl, called Elizabeth Bowes-Lyon, who came into the world on 4 August 1900 was not born to royalty, and though she married a prince called Albert they did not expect to ascend the throne, because he was not the king's eldest son.

Children born to the royal family were brought up very strictly, with the idea of preparing them for life in the public gaze.

Prince Albert as a cadet

Lady Elizabeth Bowes-Lyon at the age of seven

An unusually informal photograph (for the time) of the Bowes-Lyon family

Prince Albert was sent away to Naval college, and had a very strict upbringing. In contrast, Elizabeth's parents valued the privacy of a relaxed home life, away from publicity. So she grew up in a warm family atmosphere.

She found it natural to recreate this atmosphere with her own husband and children, and it seems clear that Albert came to value and enjoy this contrast to the way it was then thought proper to bring up a royal family.

The Queen Mother's coat of arms

If she was not born to be a Queen, this is not to say that she lacked royal blood. Robert the Bruce, the King of Scots, was one of her ancestors. Her family name was Bowes-Lyon (whose coat of arms is a pictorial pun, with bows-and-arrows and lions...), and ever since the time of 'The White Lyon', blond Sir John of the 14th century, the family has owned Glamis Castle on the edge of the Highlands.

Like all the best castles, it has its share of ghost stories. It is said that the Earl Beardie still likes to sneak up on sleeping children to shake his whiskers and rattle dice. One Lady Glamis really was burned as a witch, and Shakespeare used the castle as his setting for *Macbeth*.

Her family's roots were not only Scottish, but spread through the British Isles and beyond. In Wales they reached back to Owain Glendwr, one of the last independent warrior princes. The Bowes family gave her links to both the north and south of England, while other strands linked her to America, and even George Washington himself.

George Washington

9

Her full maiden name was Elizabeth Angela Marguerite Bowes-Lyon. It is said that she was called Elizabeth after the Queen of Shakespeare's time, that her father chose Angela since he thought she was like a little angel (one wonders what rogueries his previous eight children had got up to, if number nine seemed the first angelic one!) and Marguerite arose from her mother's fondness for flowers, something her daughter inherited.

Although the family was an affectionate one, there was a large age gap between Elizabeth and her brothers and sisters (the eldest was seventeen years older than she was). She might have become a lonely little girl, with nobody her own age to play with.

In August 1902, with her older sister (later Lady Elphinstone)

The Queen Mother's parents, the Earl and Countess of Strathmore

However, when she was just fifteen months old, she was joined in the nursery by a baby brother, David. They grew up together, almost like twins, and their mother used to call them 'her two Benjamins'. They were not always as 'angelic' as they tried to look!

A painting of Lady Elizabeth with her young brother David

11

St Paul's Walden Bury

Although they went to Glamis for part of each year, much of their childhood was spent where Elizabeth had been born: at their family home of St Paul's Walden Bury in the countryside just north of London.

The two children were encouraged to play and use their imagination. Their mother, Lady Strathmore, told them that if you found anything or anybody a bore, the fault was in yourself. However, there was little danger of boredom in the enchanted woods, full of ponds and primroses, around the Georgian house. Even the statues among the wild strawberries became characters (they called the Discus Thrower the 'Bounding Butler') while the cooing ringdoves in the big oak were dubbed Caroline-Curley-Love and Rhoda-Wrigley-Worm.

Sometimes Elizabeth and David would disappear.

When they were five and six they used to escape morning lessons by hiding in the attic of an old outhouse, where they kept a secret store of apples and chocolates. The ladder was so rotten that it would not take the weight of Nanny. They were safe from pursuit, but the fleas from the hens were a problem up there!

In fancy dress – Lady Elizabeth and her brother David, 1909

Trench warfare at Ypres, 1917

They were rogues at Glamis too. They 'defended the Castle' by pouring 'boiling oil' from the ramparts onto 'invaders'. Though it was just a tubful of cold water, it was still a bit of a shock for innocent visitors.

But soon the family was affected by the sadness of a real conflict. On Elizabeth's fourteenth birthday, the First World War broke out. Her elder brothers went away to the army, and Fergus was killed in the battle of Loos. Then Michael was reported dead too. His body was not found and David dreamed that he was still alive but badly hurt. After three months, the family received news that he was in an enemy prison hospital, with a head wound.

Lady Elizabeth shakes hands with one of the wounded soldiers who convalesced at Glamis Castle

During this time Glamis Castle became a hospital for British wounded, and Elizabeth spent most of her teenage years there, helping with the nursing. As one soldier put it, she was 'great medicine'. Lively and kindly, she sang with them, fetched messages from the village and took photographs for them to send home. She grew up quickly during the years of war, taking on more and more responsibility as her mother's health failed. Then when the Castle caught fire one dark December night, she showed that she had the nerve and leadership to cope with a full-scale emergency, too.

HMS Barham

Shortly after peace had
returned, a party was held
aboard HMS *Barham*.
Though the guests were
all very distinguished, in
the eyes of the young
midshipmen they
were also very old.
The only
visitor of
their own age
was Lady Elizabeth
Bowes-Lyon, so
there was great
competition for
her company. She asked
why one of them was
pacing the quarterdeck
with a telescope under his
arm and a worried look
on his face, instead of

joining in the dancing. Another explained that his friend was Midshipman of the Watch, and being on duty he wouldn't even get a sniff at the refreshments. 'Poor chap,' she said... and a plot was hatched. He was fed through a porthole with sandwiches and champagne, and the future Queen of England gained the devotion of several future subjects.

It was about then that the path that was to lead her to the throne began to clear before her, though she could not know that. Through Girl Guide work, she had become a friend of Princess Mary, and was invited to the Palace. There she re-met the King's second son, Prince Albert, Duke of York.

Lady Elizabeth Bowes-Lyon in Girl Guide uniform

HMS Collingwood

Elizabeth and Albert had met once before, at a children's party when she was five. He was friends with her brothers, and like them he served in the war. He was manning a gun-turret when HMS *Collingwood* fought off enemy cruisers and destroyers in the Battle of Jutland. His coolness under fire was noted both officially and unofficially (the gun-crew recalled young Albert making cocoa for them, just as usual). He enjoyed both study and sport, and as well as going to Cambridge University, he qualified

Prince Albert as a midshipman

as a pilot, and became the first royal entrant at Wimbledon.

He was a brave and capable person, but he had grown up to be a very shy boy, with a difficult stammer. What has been called the unrelieved starchiness of Court life made it difficult for the older royalty to get on with children. Lady Asquith recalls that little Bertie once tried several times to interrupt the grown-ups' conversation. King Edward VII ordered, 'Don't talk, my boy, until we have finished luncheon!' When the gruff old King finally asked what he had wanted to say, Albert had to admit, 'It doesn't matter now, Grandpapa. I was going to tell you there was a caterpillar in your salad, but you've eaten it.'

Prince Albert (right) in flying clothes

'Unrelieved starchiness' was hardly the style of the household in which Lady Elizabeth grew up, and it is clear that Prince Albert enjoyed his visits to Glamis and St Paul's Walden Bury. But the difference between her family and the stiffness of the royal household must have been something that she worried about, however much she liked

Prince Albert. On the one side was privacy and friendliness, on the other the harsh light of publicity, and very possibly loneliness. After all, it would be the first time since the 17th century that a son of a British king had married a commoner, instead of a wife who was royal in her own right.

When he first asked her to marry him, she was just twenty and she did not accept. However, two years later on the quiet Sunday morning of 14 January 1923, they strolled through winter groves in her 'enchanted woods' of St Paul's, and decided that they would get married.

The 'enchanted woods' at St Paul's Walden Bury

On the balcony – after the wedding

In the famous Glass Coach

The bride and groom, with their in-laws

Becoming a member of the royal family did bring pressures, but becoming the king's daughter-in-law worked out very happily. George V felt he had to be very strict in bringing up the princes, but since he did not expect Albert to become king, he did not have to think of her as a future queen. He was pleased to accept her as the lively girl she was.

When he died, twelve years later, it is said that she wrote to his old doctor saying that she missed him dreadfully... and that, unlike his own children, she was never afraid of him... he was always ready to listen and give advice. And when he was in the mood, she wrote, he could be deliciously funny too!

She could understand an old king whose sense of duty made him *insist* (not very successfully in her case!) that the family should never be late for breakfast... but who then allowed his pet parrot Charlotte to raid the marmalade. After all, when she was little, a bullfinch called Bobby had shared her plate (and free-flying budgerigars would later startle visitors to her own home).

Elizabeth, Duchess of York, with her father-in-law, King George V

Prince Albert was Duke of York, and as Duchess of York she was plunged with him into the extraordinarily varied round of duties of the royal family. Some of these were concerned with representing Britain to the world with solemnity and dignity, and were carried out with great seriousness. But there was a less solemn side too. Part of the success of the royal family in helping to bind together the United Kingdom and Commonwealth for so much of the 20th century came from the lead that she helped to give in sharing friendliness and humour in a way that ordinary families appreciated. This was less easy than it seemed, because even then the constant pursuit by journalists and the publicity over their every action made it difficult to be at all natural, particularly for a shy person like Prince Albert.

But as the old King wrote to him, 'You are indeed a lucky man... I am quite certain that Elizabeth will be a splendid partner in your work...' and so it proved.

Glamorous for a formal occasion

24

Trying her hand at a coconut shy   *A wounded soldier jokes with her*

She helped him to overcome his stutter. But more importantly, her own character soon shone through, and broke the ice for them both with the public.

*The ceremony of 'Crossing the Line' (the Equator) on HMS Renown –
even the Duke and Duchess must submit to the fun!*

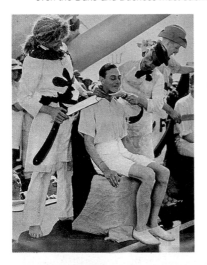

At the Wembley Exhibition in 1925

At Darlington

They were soon meeting the public all over Britain and all round the world, in their role as Royal ambassadors. Travel by land, sea and air became a constant feature of her life. The couple were amongst the first of the royal family to take regularly to the air. At first this was in canvas-covered biplanes, but in later life Elizabeth was to try her hand at the controls of a jet in the stratosphere, and to have grandsons who flew helicopters and 1600 kph jet fighters.

Arriving at Edinburgh Airport

The Duchess takes to the air for the first time

The Royal Yacht Britannia

But much of her travel was at a more sedate rate, and amid the hurly-burly of public engagements, she must have appreciated the chance of a little peace and privacy that she could enjoy on the Royal Yacht, or on some (though not all!) trains.

On Britannia – the sitting room

The Duke of York drives a model train at a bazaar

On the lawn at Windsor

Their first daughter, who was to become Queen Elizabeth, was born in London on 21 April 1926, and their second, Princess Margaret Rose, at Glamis on 21 August 1930. This meant that they were eleven and six years old before their father and mother were unexpectedly made king and queen. Instead of taking Court life as their model, their parents looked on family life as a sanctuary in which people could develop despite the pressures on them in the outside world.

The happiness of her own early days seems to have guided the way she and her husband decided to bring up their own family. This proved important, because the pattern of family life that she set with Albert then, in the ten years before they were aware that they would come to the throne, was carried through into their reign.

With Princess Elizabeth and the Earl of Airlie

At Royal Lodge, Windsor

This feeling of her royal family being a real family contributed a lot to the way that their popularity endured with many people for so much of the 20th century.

Relaxing at Windsor

When the old king died on 20 January 1936, his oldest son was proclaimed King Edward VIII. But he was never to be crowned. In the face of great hostility from politicians and others over his chosen wife, he decided to abdicate: that is, to give up his right to the throne.

So, quite suddenly Prince Albert found that he was required to become a sovereign. He was to be known as King George VI, and his wife would become his Queen Consort.

They were crowned in Westminster Abbey on 12 May 1937. The two little princesses were there, dressed in white and gold, and appeared afterwards with their parents on the balcony of Buckingham Palace.

A solemn moment

After the coronation in 1937 – a balcony appearance

At Buckingham Palace, World War II

They all had to put a brave face on it, but the change was not of their choosing. The new king had not gone through the training of a Prince of Wales, and he told Lord Mountbatten he felt quite unprepared to take over the affairs of state. However, as his brother had said during his abdication speech, '...he has one matchless blessing... not bestowed on me – a happy home life.' And as he came to the throne, he left no doubt of the value he set on this: 'With my wife and helpmate by my side, I take up the heavy task which lies before me.'

They needed all their family fortitude, for soon the country was looking to them to inspire steadfastness and hope through the long years of the Second World War. The king and queen refused to leave the capital, though the Palace was hit nine times by bomb and rocket attacks.

1 *The queen takes bananas to children injured in a bombing raid*
2 *The king and queen tour East London in 1945*
3 *Inspecting the damage to Buckingham Palace*
4 *The queen talks to two Canadian soldiers*
5 *With Winston Churchill on Victory Day 1945*

1947 – This royal family group included Lieutenant Philip Mountbatten, Princess Elizabeth's fiancé

By the time the war ended in 1945, King George and Queen Elizabeth could be in no doubt that they had earned the affection of their people. This was a happy period for the whole family. First, Princess Elizabeth married the young Philip Mountbatten, who became the Duke of Edinburgh. Then in April of 1948, her parents celebrated their own Silver Wedding, before their first grandchild, Prince Charles, was born in November. The second grandchild, Princess Anne, arrived in August 1950.

A Silver Wedding picture

The king found as much pleasure with his grandchildren as he had with his own daughters. But serious illness had troubled him ever since he was a boy, and although he was still only in his fifties, problems with leg arteries and then a malignant lung growth weakened him seriously. Besides taking over many of his royal duties, his wife worked with the nurses and doctors. She helped to see him through days and

nights of crisis, just as she had helped others with the nursing so long before, when she was a girl at Glamis.

A happy afternoon on the moors in 1949

The funeral of King George VI at Windsor Castle

King George VI died in February 1952, leaving Elizabeth a widow at just fifty-one years of age. As Queen Consort, a commoner married to a king, she did not succeed him. So it was her daughter who came to the throne, through the blood royal of her father the late king. Because they both were Elizabeths, the parent henceforth became known officially as Her Majesty Queen Elizabeth The Queen Mother – and as years went by, unofficially (though certainly not unaffectionately) as the Queen Mum…

The Castle of Mey

The Queen Mother had not expected to become a queen at all, and in the sadness following her husband's death she might have retreated into the kind of quiet country life she had enjoyed as a child. When she started making a home out of the old Castle of Mey, in one of the furthest corners of her native Scotland, people wondered if she were going to retire there for good.

However, once the first sorrow had passed she set out, as she put it, to continue the work that she and her husband had sought to do together. Winston Churchill had been to see her at Balmoral, and it is believed they talked about duty, and joy.

In the years that followed, the affection in which the Queen Mother was held by people in Britain and many other parts of the world ensured that she was kept busy. Although she was involved in an extraordinary range of activities, she always managed to approach events small and large (from chats with individuals to great formal occasions) with her own pleasant and highly personal style.

1   Opening a biology laboratory at Queen Mary College
2   At Belfast University
3   Presenting a shamrock to the Irish Guards
4   At the Royal Opera House, Covent Garden
5   Meeting pop stars
6   At the opera
7   An unexpected skill!
8   At Dover, as Warden of the Cinque Ports

This portrait was painted for the Royal College of Music by Sir Leonard Boden

At her desk

Her ability to set people at their ease, so that they genuinely enjoyed chatting with her, was not just a reflection of her natural personality. It was also the result of quite a lot of homework on whom she was meeting, what they did and what their own particular interests were. Down the years, her behind-the-scenes work also included innumerable private business meetings with people from the charitable organisations which she helped. In the light of all this it is remarkable how many public engagements she managed to undertake.

Even in 1991 she made a hundred public appearances, and she did not stop there. Even further into her nineties, she still managed almost as many. Remember that each public event involved not only the appearance itself, but the time and stress for a person of her age in travelling back and forth across the kingdom. Many organisations wanted her portrait painted, so even periods of repose were turned to use, as she sat patiently for artists.

At Norwich Airport

With husband and family, at Royal Lodge, Windsor, in 1940

It can't be easy for anyone to live with pressure like this, not only for year after year, but for decade after decade. She had her own favourite forms of relaxation. Not surprisingly, after the special magic of those 'enchanted woods' of Walden Bury, gardens and flowers were something that she cared deeply about.

In her golf mobile at Sandringham Flower Show

She and Albert spent some of their happiest times together remodelling the garden of the Royal Lodge at Windsor, which remained a beloved place for her all her life. Her enjoyment and knowledge of plants was very apparent in her visits to events such as the Chelsea Flower Show, and a number of roses were named after her.

Gardening was not her only outdoor form of relaxation. For well over half a century, she enjoyed fishing. The thousands of anglers in Britain know just how restorative a day out with a rod can be... even if it does rain! She had been an

Fishing in New Zealand, in 1927

angler since her girlhood in Scotland, and when Prince Charles was a boy, she taught him fly fishing, too. It was ironic that two of the very few medical emergencies in her life were caused by fish bones lodged in her throat.

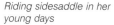
Riding sidesaddle in her young days

A pat for her winning horse

Another enthusiasm which ran right through her life was for horses. When she was a child, her tiny Shetland pony, Bobs, sometimes found his way indoors (and indeed upstairs…). Even as a great-grandmother, she had a lively interest in the training of racehorses. Her horses won over 400 National Hunt Races, and the Queen Mother Champion Steeplechase was named in her honour. She loved dogs as well as horses, and corgis were her constant companions.

Receiving her Honorary Doctorate of Music

She found relaxation of another kind in music. She was the most musical of the Royal Family, and in 1994 she was awarded an Honorary Doctorate of Music by the Royal Scottish Academy of Music and Drama. But her taste was not only for the classics. From her youth at Glamis onwards, she enjoyed Scottish folksongs... and dancing. When she was well into her eighties, Lord Thurso (her neighbour at Castle Mey) invited her to a Highland Ball and she danced until long after midnight.

Inevitably, as the years passed she became frailer, but her enduring liveliness of spirit had much to do with the affection she continued to inspire in many people. This was reflected in the celebrations marking her 95th birthday.

As a small girl, with her brother and dancing master

Enjoying a lively Scottish country dance

A moment shared with former Prime Minister John Major

That year, 1995, also brought the fiftieth anniversary of the end of Second World War. VE ('Victory-Europe') and VJ ('Victory-Japan') events marked this. In 1989, she had crossed the Channel to Normandy, for the forty-fifth anniversary of the D-Day landings which led ultimately to the end of the war.

As then, the 1995 commemorations were a blend of celebrations for what had been achieved, and sadness for the high cost in lives and suffering.

Remembered sadness

At the Drumhead Service during D-Day celebrations

The Queen Mother's participation in these events was received warmly and her steadfastness in wartime had not been forgotten. Then, her image of kindliness and concern amid the rubble of the blitz seemed to many to symbolise values worth fighting for, especially when set against the harsh fanaticism of Hitler.

Those of her own generation remembered that this was not the only war where she had shared grief. With brothers killed and wounded in the First World War, it had been no mere formality for her to go to the service held in Westminster Abbey in 1993, to mark the seventy-fifth anniversary of the Armistice which brought peace in 1918.

Outside Westminster Abbey at the 75th Anniversary of the signing of Armistice

A toast to a great lady

Throughout her long life, the public image of the lady who came to be known as the 'Queen Mum' was one of charm and kindliness. Lady Furness remarked she was the woman she would most like as a next-door neighbour.

By 1993, Sir Edward Ford described her as 'perhaps the most loved person in the Western World'. But to have come to the monarchy from the outside, and

Surrounded by children on her 95th birthday

Ruth, Lady Fermoy (above) and Sir Martin Gilliat, her Personal Private Secretary (below), each spent 37 years in the service of the Queen Mother

then played such a part in shaping it through so much of the 20th century, implies considerable strength of character. Lord Halifax regarded her as 'a steel hand – within a velvet glove'. As one newspaper put it, 'She is much more than everyone's lovable old granny. She is a woman of greatness...'

But it seems that strength and humanity were not incompatible. If her private character had been very different from her public face, one would have expected frequent turnover in her personal staff. On the contrary, several served with her for over thirty years. This surely says a lot about the Queen Mother's personality.

Visiting bomb-damage in London in 1941

   Queen Elizabeth The Queen Mother was the longest-serving Queen Dowager in the history of Great Britain. Some of the wounded soldiers she helped to nurse at Glamis during the First World War had been born in the late nineteenth century. Even those who were just babies when she and King George VI endured the Second World War bombing along with their people are now over their half-century mark. When the Queen Mother was born in 1900, Queen Victoria still reigned, and much has happened since then. With population increasing so rapidly around the globe and whole new technologies developing, the nature of human society has changed in many ways during her lifetime. It is said that a week is a long time in politics, and certainly, on some matters, people's views can alter very rapidly indeed.

Going supersonic – by Concorde

At a carnival in 1924 in aid of the 'Save the Children' Fund

In the year 2000, as the nation celebrated the arrival of a new millennium, the Queen Mother celebrated her 100th birthday. At a time when people were celebrating change and new ideals, the Queen Mother's century-long life served as a reminder that some values such as grace, dignity and respect, can be passed on and cherished from generation to generation. The affection in which she was held by all marks her success not just as a royal, but also as a person.

The royal family at Clarence House for the Queen Mother's birthday.

Family Tree

PATRICK (LYON),
3rd EARL of STRATHMORE & KINGHORNE
Born 1643
Died 1695

Lady HELEN MIDDLETON
Married 1662
Died 1708

JOHN (LYON),
4th EARL of STRATHMORE & KINGHORNE
Born 1663
Died 1712

Lady ELIZABETH STANHOPE
Married 1691
Died 1723

THOMAS (LYON),
8th EARL of STRATHMORE & KINGHORNE
Born 1704
Died 1753

JEAN NICHOLSON
Married 1736
Died 1778

JOHN (LYON),
9th EARL of STRATHMORE & KINGHORNE
Born 1737
Died 1776

MARY ELEANOR BOWES
Married 1767
Died 1800

THOMAS (BOWES-LYON),
11th EARL of STRATHMORE & KINGHORNE
Born 1773
Died 1846

MARY ELIZABETH CARPENTER
Married 1800
Died 1811